ALL ABOUT FOOD

FRUIT

Cecilia Fitzsimons

Silver Burdett Press
Parsippany, New Jersey

First American publication
1997 by Silver Burdett Press
A Division of Simon & Schuster
299 Jefferson Road,
Parsippany, NJ 07054-0480

A ZOË BOOK

Produced by
Zoë Books Limited
15 Worthy Lane
Winchester
Hampshire SO23 7AB
England

Editors: Kath Davies, Imogen Dawson
Design: Sterling Associates
Illustrations: Cecilia Fitzsimons
Production: Grahame Griffiths

First published in Great Britain in 1996 by
Zoë Books Limited
15 Worthy Lane
Winchester
Hampshire SO23 7AB

Printed in Belgium by Proost N.V.
1 2 3 4 5 6 7 8 9 10

Library of Congress Cataloging-in-Publication Data

Fitzsimons, Cecilia
Fruit/Cecilia Fitzsimons.
    p. cm.—(All about food)
"A Zoë book"
Includes index.
    Summary: Provides information about various kinds of fruits
as well as some advice on growing them and activities and recipes
using them.
    ISBN 0-382-39592-1 (LSB) ISBN 0-382-39597-2 (PBK)
    1. Fruit—Juvenile literature. 2. Cookery (Fruit)—Juvenile
Literature. 3. Fruit—culture—Juvenile Literature. [1. Fruit.]
I. Title. II. Series.
TX397.F57 1996   95-5065
641.3'4—dc 20   CIP
                                          AC

Contents

Introduction

Thousands of years ago people wandered from place to place in search of food. They hunted wild animals, and they gathered seeds, nuts, and fruits. They shared the food with their family and friends.

About 10,000 years ago, people began to settle in one place, instead of moving around. They found out how to grow wheat, beans, and other food crops, including fruits.

People also discovered many different ways of keeping, or **preserving**, fruits. They learned to store some fruits in cool places, to dry fruits, to make jams, jellies, and drinks with fruit juice. Today fruits are also canned, bottled, frozen, and chilled.

Fruit facts

The southern half of the earth is called the Southern **Hemisphere**. It is summer there when it is winter in the Northern Hemisphere.

When fruits have stopped growing, or go out of season, in the Northern Hemisphere, they come into season in the Southern Hemisphere.

Fruits are shipped and flown across the world. They are in stores all year round.

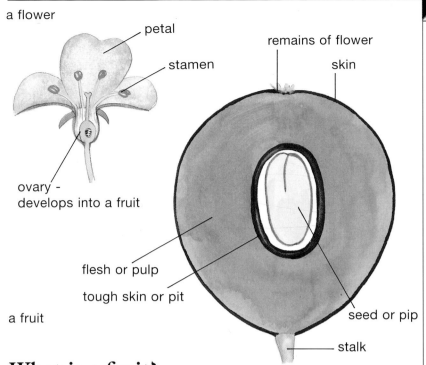

a flower

petal

stamen

ovary -
develops into a fruit

remains of flower

skin

flesh or pulp

tough skin or pit

a fruit

seed or pip

stalk

What is a fruit?

Plants flower, then set seeds, which grow into new plants. But plants cannot move. They must find a way to carry their seeds away from the parent plant. Fruits contain seeds. Brightly colored, tasty fruits attract animals and birds. They eat the fruit and spread the seeds.

A fruit develops from a flower. It usually has layers of skin and flesh inside, which are one or more seeds.

In the kitchen

You will find easy-to-follow recipes for different fruits in this book. Here are some points to remember when you prepare food:

1. Sharp knives, hot liquids, and pans are dangerous. *Always ask an adult* to help you when you are preparing or cooking food in the kitchen.

2. Before you start, put on an apron and wash your hands.

3. All the ingredients and equipment are listed at the beginning of each recipe. Make sure that you have everything you need before you start.

4. Read the instructions. Measure or weigh all the ingredients very carefully.

Think green

We often throw away things that we could use again, or **recycle**. If we reused some of our newspapers, cans, bottles, and plastic packaging, we would help to improve our **environment**.

Many fruits are wrapped in packages when they are sold. When you read this book, you will find some ideas for things that you can do and make, using fruits and their packages.

Grow your own fruit

Many fruit plants can be grown at home. You will find instructions to help you grow them when you read this book.

Here are some tips to help you to grow healthy plants. You can buy young plants from garden centers, or grow them yourself from seeds and **cuttings**.

All plants need soil, water, and sunlight for strong, healthy growth.

Planting in a pot

1. Take a clean plant pot. Place a few small stones over the holes in the bottom of the pot. This helps water to drain through the pot.

2. Fill the pot with potting soil. Make a hole in the middle of the soil. Gently put in your plant or seedling, taking care not to damage its stem or roots.

3. Push the soil down around the roots. Add more soil and press it down firmly.

4. Water the plant well and allow the soil to drain.

5. Place the pot in a saucer, dish, or pot holder to catch any water. Stand it on a sunny window ledge or other well-lighted place.

6. Water the plant regularly. Once a week is usually enough. Occasionally feed it with plant food, bought from a garden center. Follow the instructions on the bottle or packet.

Planting in the garden

Many plants can be grown in the garden.

1. Dig a hole and put some well-rotted **compost** in the bottom of it.

2. Tap the bottom of your plant pot first to loosen the plant's roots. Remove the plant from its pot.

3. Gently place the plant in the hole. Replace the soil around the roots and press down firmly with your foot. Water and feed the plant regularly.

Seeds

You can buy some seeds from garden centers and mail-order catalogs. Follow the instructions printed on each packet.

Seeds from fresh fruits

You can also collect seeds from fresh fruits. This often works well, although some seeds may not grow, or **germinate**. Collecting seeds doesn't cost much and can produce rare and exciting plants.

Collecting seeds

1. Simply remove the seeds from the fruit and plant them. (See page 9.)

2. If the seeds are in a soft, sticky fruit flesh, or **pulp**, wash them in a strainer to remove the pulp.

3. Dry the seeds on a paper towel before planting.

4. Dried seeds can often be stored in an airtight jar for months.

melon seeds

water

Think green

Use compost made of leaves rather than dried peat to help save bogs and wetlands.

Grow seeds and plants in margarine tubs and yogurt containers. Make a hole in the bottom to let the water drain through.

Place clear plastic boxes or bottles (cut off the bottom first) over each young plant to make a mini-greenhouse. This will keep slugs away, too.

soft drink bottle

yogurt container

Apples and pears

Apples are the world's most popular fruit. More than 1,500 different types, or **varieties**, are grown in orchards across the world. Each country has its own favorite varieties. Sweet apples are often eaten raw. Apples are also cooked in many dishes.

Sweet apple juice is used in many fruit drinks. The juice of small, bitter cider apples is **fermented** to make cider and vinegar. **Distilled** vinegar is used to preserve foods.

apple

Pears are related to apples. There are more than a thousand varieties of pears. Soft pears are eaten raw. Hard pears are often cooked.

Europeans use perry pears to make pear cider, called perry.

pear

Fruit facts

Farmed, or **cultivated**, apples are all descended from wild crab apples that grow in Northern Europe, Asia, and America.

Apple trees can grow up to 40ft (12m) high.

The U.S. crop of apples is about 4,427,000 metric tons a year.

Pear trees can grow to 60ft (18m) and may be 300 years old.

Pear wood is hard and can be used to make furniture.

Grow your own tree

1. You can grow an apple or a pear tree from seed. When you have finished eating the fruit, collect the seeds from the core.

2. Fill a pot with potting soil and plant a seed in the top. Cover the seed with soil and water it well.

3. Cover the pot with a plastic bag and leave it near a sunny window.

4. When the seedling appears, remove the plastic bag. Stand the pot in a dish or saucer. Water it once a week.

5. As your tree grows bigger, **transplant** it into a bigger pot. Eventually it will need to be planted in the soil outside.

Think green

Some apples and pears are packed in strong cardboard boxes that contain sheets of **molded** packaging. Ask the storekeeper if you can have a box and the packaging so that you can reuse it.

Making furniture

You can use fruit boxes to store things such as toys.

If you turn a box on its side, you can make a bookcase.

You could paint the outside of each box with different colors and patterns.

Make a game

You can also use one sheet of molded packaging to make this game. (To play it, you will need marbles as well.)

1. Paint the inside of each mold a different color.

2. Write or paint different numbers on the inside of each mold.

3. Toss marbles into the molds and aim for the highest score.

Oranges, lemons, and limes

Orange trees are small. They have leathery leaves and white, waxy flowers with a strong fragrance. The fruits are large and juicy, with a sweet-sour taste. The fruit flesh is divided into parts, or **segments**, and contains the seeds.

Oranges are often eaten fresh or used in salads. Bitter oranges are used to make marmalade. Orange juice is sold fresh, or is canned or frozen to preserve it. There are more than 80 varieties of oranges. Tangerines, mandarins, and satsumas are small oranges. They are eaten fresh, or the segments are canned. Kumquats are tiny fruits that are eaten whole.

orange

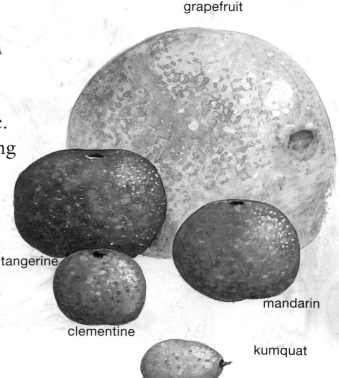

grapefruit

tangerine

clementine

mandarin

kumquat

Clementines were first produced by **crossing** a wild orange with a tangerine. Grapefruit were developed by crossing a wild fruit called a pomelo with an orange. Ugli (tangelo) fruit is a cross between a grapefruit and a tangerine.

ugli fruit

lemon

Lemon trees have small, pointed, yellow fruit. The juice is sour, or **acidic**, and has a strong flavor.

lime

lemon squeezer

lemonade

Limes are small green fruits, which grow in hot, wet, **tropical** countries.

Lime and lemon juice is used to make drinks, for cooking, and for making jams

Fruit facts

Orange trees first grew in China. Oranges were taken to Europe by Arab traders more than 1,000 years ago.

A medium-sized orange contains the amount of **vitamin** C that a healthy adult should eat daily.

Lemons, oranges, and limes are all **citrus** fruits. Their juices contain citric acid.

Grated lemon peel is called **zest**. It is used as a flavoring.

British sailors were given lime juice to keep them from getting an illness called scurvy. They were known as "Limeys."

Make a lemon battery

You will need:

4 lemons

5 pieces of copper wire with ends stripped

1 small light bulb (1.5v)

4 nails

1. Connect a nail to the end of a piece of wire. Push the nail into a lemon. Repeat with three other nails, wires, and lemons.

2. Push the copper end of the first piece of wire into the second lemon. Use the next two pieces of wire to connect the other lemons together in the same way.

3. Push one end of the fifth wire into the first lemon.

4. Connect the ends of the wires from the first and last lemons to the light bulb.

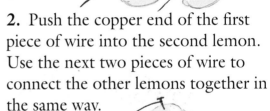

The bulb will light up, if you have connected every item together carefully. How does the lemon battery work?

Bananas

Bananas grow in tropical countries. The banana plant is a giant **herb** that grows from a stem under the ground. Some banana plants are 25 ft (8m) tall.

When the banana plant is a year old, a flowering stem grows down from the top of it. The flowers develop into seedless bananas. Each stem may hold 200 bananas, arranged in "hands."

Banana plants are unusual because no **pollination** takes place. The main stem of the banana plant dies when the fruiting has finished. New plants develop from the shoots, or **suckers**, at the bottom of the plant stem.

When the bananas have been harvested, the farmer cuts down the banana plant. It is chopped up and left to turn into compost for the next crop. One good sucker is left to grow into the new tree.

Most bananas are picked when they are still green. They are sent to different countries, or **exported**, by ship. Bananas ripen slowly. They are stored until they are ripe and ready to be sold.

banana plant

bananas

Most bananas are eaten raw, but some are cooked. Bananas can also be dried, ground into flour, and fermented for vinegar.

Plantain plants are part of the same family as bananas. Their large, fleshy fruits are cooked as a vegetable in many tropical countries.

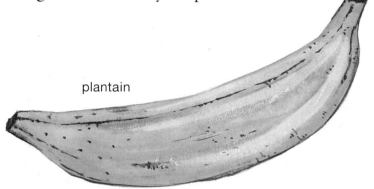

plantain

Fruit facts

People in the tropics have eaten bananas for thousands of years.

There are more than 100 varieties of bananas. Some have red skins.

Bananas contain high levels of sugars, **starch**, and vitamins A and C.

Banana ash is used to make soap.

Think green

Bananas can be grown on newly cleared forest land. Some farmers are cutting down the rain forest to grow bananas. This practice destroys the homes of many types of plants and animals. Some of them will be lost forever. Find out where bananas are grown before you buy them.

Banana milkshake

You will need:

1 ripe banana

1 pt (500 ml) milk

a bowl

a fork

a spoon

a large container with a tightly fitting lid

a tall glass

1. Put the banana in the bowl and mash it up with a fork.

2. Spoon the mashed banana into the container and add the milk.

3. Put the lid on the container and make sure that it is secure.

4. Shake the container until the banana and milk are mixed together. The milk should be frothy.

5. Pour the milkshake into a glass and drink it.

Pineapples

The pineapple plant has tough, leathery leaves. Each leaf looks like a sword, and can be as long as 3ft (90cm). The leaves often have sharp, jagged edges, which can make picking pineapples very painful! A round ball, made up of hundreds of tiny purple flowers, grows in the middle of the pineapple plant. Each flower forms a berrylike fruit. These fruits all join together and grow into one large pineapple.

Pineapples first came to Europe from South America. Now they are grown in most tropical countries.

Pineapples are one of the most popular tropical fruits. About 503,000 metric tons of pineapples are produced in Hawaii every year.

You can buy fresh or canned pineapples. They are also used to make fruit juice and jam.

Fruit facts

Pine-apple was the old name for pine cones that grow on pine trees. Because the pineapple looks like a huge cone, it, too, was called a pine-apple.

Pineapples contain an **enzyme** that is used in blood tests.

Fibers in pineapple leaves are used to make rope and a cloth called pino.

Pineapples are related to rain-forest plants called bromeliads, which are sometimes grown as houseplants.

Grow your own pineapples

You can grow pineapples by planting the leafy shoots that sprout from the top and bottom of the fruit.

1. Twist off the leafy shoot from the top of a fresh pineapple. Clean away any flesh that remains on the shoot.

2. Pull off a few rows of leaves from the bottom of the shoot. On the stem you will see rows of brown spots that will grow into the roots of your plant.

3. Plant the shoot in a pot containing potting soil. Water the shoot and cover it with a plastic bag. Leave the shoot in a warm, lighted place for about four weeks.

4. Remove the plastic bag and put your pineapple plant in a sunny, warm place. Do not give it too much water. Your plant should grow well at home, but unless you put it in a hot greenhouse, it will not produce fruits.

Fabulous fruit salad

You will need:

1 large ripe pineapple

1 teaspoon of sugar

1 apple, 1 pear, 1 peach

A few strawberries, raspberries, or cherries

---

1 large mixing bowl

1 sharp knife

1 cutting board

1 wooden spoon

plastic film wrap

Method

1. Wash and dry the pineapple.

2. *Ask an adult* to: cut the pineapple in half with a sharp knife; cut out and throw away the tough core that runs through the middle; cut and scoop out the rest of the pineapple's flesh.

3. Put the pieces into a large bowl. You will be left with two empty, bowl-shaped pineapple shells.

4. Wash the other fruits and dry them. *Ask an adult* to take out the cores, pits, and stalks. Then slice them, using a sharp knife.

5. Put these fruits in the bowl with the pineapple pieces. Add the sugar. Gently mix everything together.

6. Spoon the fruit mixture into the pineapple shells. Cover the shells with plastic film wrap and put them into the refrigerator until you are ready to eat them.

Strawberries and raspberries

strawberry

Fresh strawberries and raspberries are in **season** for only a short time each summer in North America and Northern Europe. Fresh fruit from other countries is in the shops all year round, but it is often expensive.

Strawberries

flower

The fruit grows on small, white-flowered plants. The plants spread by seeds or by sending out shoots called runners, whose tips then grow roots and a new plant. A strawberry is not a true fruit because the seeds are found on the surface of the fruit, not inside it.

Strawberries are best eaten raw with cream, yogurt, or ice cream. They can also be cooked or used to make jams, drinks, and food flavorings.

strawberry plant

runner

raspberry cane

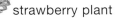

raspberry

Raspberries

Raspberries grow on tall, straight **canes** up to 6ft (1.8m) tall. They also have white flowers. The fruits are made up of a cluster of juicy **drupelets**, each containing a seed.

You can buy fresh, canned, or frozen raspberries. They can be eaten raw or cooked. Raspberries are also used to make jams, jellies, and drinks.

Grow your own strawberries

Strawberries can be grown from seed or by planting the young plants that grow at the tip of runners.

Put each plant straight into soil in the garden or in a pot filled with potting soil. Water each plant well.

Fruit facts

Straw is put under strawberries to protect the fruit, but they probably got their name from the Anglo-Saxon word *streawberige*, which means "spreading berry."

Most raspberries are red, but some varieties are white, yellow, or black.

Raspberries may have been named after a sixteenth-century French wine called raspis. Raspberries used to be called hindberries.

Think green

Strawberries and raspberries are often sold in small baskets. You can reuse the empty baskets to store things or as gift baskets. You can paint or decorate wooden baskets. Plastic baskets are good containers for growing seeds. You can paint them with plastic modeling paints.

Berry easy flan

You will need:

1 sponge cake flan shell

1 large container of plain yogurt or whipped cream

1 small basket of raspberries or strawberries

1 teaspoon of sugar

---

1 strainer

1 tablespoon

1 serving plate

Method

1. Twist off any leaves from the fruit. Then wash the fruit quickly but gently in cold water. Leave the fruit to drain in the strainer.

2. Put the flan shell on a serving dish. Use a spoon to cover the bottom of the flan shell with a thick layer of yogurt or whipped cream.

3. Spoon the fruit on top of the yogurt or cream.

4. Sprinkle the fruit with sugar and serve.

Peaches and plums

Peaches, plums, apricots, cherries, and their relatives belong to the plant family called *Prunus*. These fruit trees are covered in beautiful blossom in springtime. The white or pink flowers produce large, juicy fruits. Inside each fruit is a single seed which has a hard case or pit.

You can buy these fruits fresh, canned, dried, or frozen. They can be eaten raw or cooked. Fresh peaches are eaten as a delicacy. They are also used to make jam. The fruit juice can be used to make soft drinks.

Peaches and apricots were first grown in China. Now they grow in many areas where the climate is warm.

Peaches have a juicy white or yellow flesh, reddish velvety skin, and a large wrinkled pit. Nectarines are a smooth-skinned variety of peach. Apricots are small and orange, with a furry skin.

There are many varieties of plums, such as Victoria plums, damsons, and greengages. Dried plums are called prunes.

peach

peach blossom

apricot

nectarine

prune

damson

greengage

Victoria plum

18

cherry

Cherries are small, round fruits, each carried on a long stalk. Their skin is shiny, and is dark red to yellowish in color. Most cherries have sweet, juicy flesh. Some, such as the morello, are sour and are used in cooking or to make jams and drinks.

Fruit facts

Peaches and apricots are rich in vitamins A and C.

Apricots were first grown in China more than 4,000 years ago.

The wild plum of Northern Europe is the sloe. Sloes have small, hard, bitter fruits.

Round cherry pits were used to play games such as marbles.

Almonds are the nutlike seeds from a fruit that looks like a green apricot.

Peach Melba

(first made for the Australian singer Nellie Melba)

You will need: (for 4 people)

2 fresh peaches or 1 can of peach halves

1 pint of vanilla ice cream

1 small basket of raspberries

3 tablespoons of confectioners sugar

---

1 strainer

1 sharp knife

can opener

1 mixing bowl

1 wooden spoon

1 tablespoon

4 small serving bowls

Method

1. Wash the raspberries quickly but gently in cold water. Leave the fruit to drain in the strainer.

2. *Ask an adult* to help you to cut the fresh peaches in half, using a sharp knife, or to open the can of peaches for you.

3. Put the strainer of raspberries over the mixing bowl. Stir the fruit with a wooden spoon, squashing it through the strainer to make a puree in the bowl below. Throw away the seeds.

4. Measure the confectioners sugar. Slowly add it to the raspberry puree. Stir the mixture well.

5. Put a scoop or thick slice of ice cream in each of the four serving dishes.

6. If you are using canned peaches, drain the juice. Then put a peach half, flat side down, on top of each portion of ice cream in the serving dishes.

7. Spoon the raspberry puree on top of the peach in each dish and serve immediately.

More berries

This mixed group of berries comes from the cooler parts of Northern Europe, Asia, and North America. Many of them still grow wild. The fruits are small and often sour, but they taste good when they are cooked. They are also used to make jams, jellies, and drinks. You can buy these fruits fresh, canned, bottled, or frozen.

Blackberries, or brambles, grow wild in woods and uncultivated fields. The long, sprawling stems have sharp thorns, although some cultivated varieties are thornless. When a stem touches the ground, it grows roots to form a new plant. The black, raspberry-like fruits develop from clusters of white or pink flowers.

Loganberries were first grown in California by Judge J. H. Logan in 1881, by crossbreeding a raspberry with a blackberry. Tayberries are similar and were developed in Scotland.

blackberry

loganberry

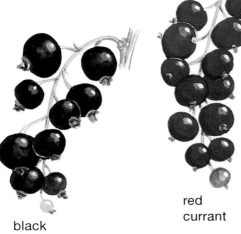

black currant

red currant

white currant

Currants are small shrubs with strong-smelling leaves. Sprays of small flowers produce round berries with seeds, or pips, in a juicy pulp. Red currants and white currants are sweeter than black currants. They are often eaten raw with cream.

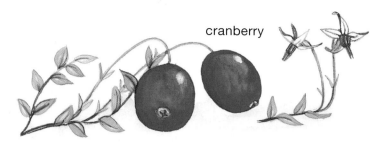
cranberry

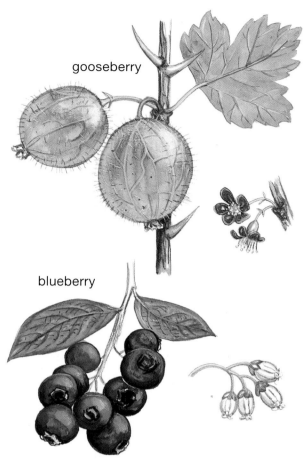
gooseberry

blueberry

Cranberries grow wild on heaths, bogs, and swampy ground. They are also cultivated in North America.

Gooseberries are large, hairy currants, which are green, yellow, or pinkish in color. Gooseberry bushes are small, and the branches are often very prickly.

Blueberries are fruits of large shrubs that grow well on poor soils. They are planted in areas of North America and Spain where little else will grow. Bilberries, huckleberries, and whortleberries are similar fruits.

Fruit facts

Blackberry juice was used to dye cloth navy blue and indigo.

Black currants are rich in vitamins C and B. Their juice may be used to soothe sore throats and colds.

Pemmican is a Native American cake of dried meat flavored with dried currants.

The gooseberry is called the "mackerel currant" in French because gooseberry sauce is served with mackerel, a type of fish.

Cranberry sauce is served with turkey for the traditional Thanksgiving dinner.

Blueberry pie is a traditional dish in North America.

Think green

Ask your family if you can pick some wild fruits when they are in season. Then you could help to cook or preserve them.

Save glass jars with strong screw-top lids. You can reuse the jars for homemade jams, jellies, and pickles.

Melons

Melons grow on low, spreading plants. Like their relatives—cucumbers, zucchini, marrows, and pumpkins—melons have huge fruits that develop beneath large yellow flowers. They have a thick skin or rind, watery flesh, and a mass of seeds in a central cavity. The ancient Egyptians grew melons, and today they are grown in many warm and tropical countries.

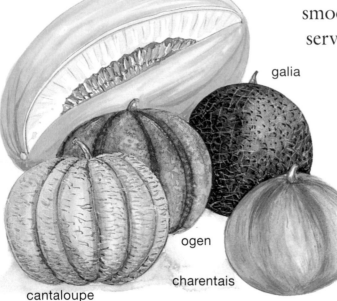

honeydew

galia

ogen

charentais

cantaloupe

There are many varieties of melons. Honeydew melons are grown in warm climates. They are oval shaped with a smooth skin. They are eaten fresh, or served with sugar, ginger, or nutmeg. Galia, cantaloupe, ogen, and charentais are smaller, round melons, often with a wrinkled skin. They are also grown in warm climates. Their juicy orange flesh has a rich, fruity smell when the fruit is ripe. To choose the best fruit, smell the base of the melon. Only ripe melons smell good.

Watermelons are related to climbing plants that probably came from tropical Africa. They are now grown in warm and tropical countries worldwide. The huge fruits can grow to 40 lb (18kg) in weight.

Watermelons have bright red, watery flesh, which is extremely juicy and thirst-quenching. Their dark-colored seeds contain oils and can be eaten. The green rind and the hard flesh found just beneath the rind is cooked and made into jams and pickles.

watermelon

22

Think green

Collect, wash, and dry melon seeds from different kinds of melons. Then you can reuse the melon seeds to make other things. Here are a few ideas.

1. Use a needle and strong thread to string the melon seeds together. You could make a necklace or a bracelet out of them.

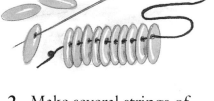

2. Make several strings of melon seeds. Join the strings together and copy the patterns in these pictures to make a mat.

glue

3. Make a picture out of melon seeds. First draw your picture on a stiff piece of card. Then glue the seeds onto it, to finish your picture.

Shrimp and melon salad

You will need:

½ head of lettuce

½ honeydew melon

6oz (175g) peeled shrimp

6 oz (175g) Cheddar cheese

½ lemon

1 teaspoon freshly chopped parsley

1 serving dish

1 sharp knife

cutting board

1 tablespoon

1 large mixing bowl

Method

1. Separate the lettuce leaves. Wash them and shake them dry. Arrange the leaves in the serving dish.

2. *Ask an adult* to cut the melon into slices, using a sharp knife. Scoop out the seeds with a spoon.

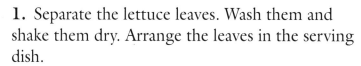

3. *Ask an adult* to cut the rind off each slice and to cut the slices into cubes. Put the melon cubes into a large mixing bowl.

4. *Ask an adult* to cut the cheese into cubes. Then add the cheese cubes and the shrimp to the melon cubes. Gently mix everything together.

5. Carefully spoon the mixture onto the lettuce leaves. Then squeeze the juice from the lemon over the salad.

6. *Ask an adult* to chop up the parsley leaves. Then sprinkle the parsley over the salad and serve.

Fruits of the vine

A vine is a long, trailing plant that climbs up and over other plants, often clinging onto them with tightly coiled **tendrils**.

Grapevines have long stems that become quite woody with age. Clusters of tiny flowers develop into grapes, which are red, blue, green or black, depending on the variety.

Grapes are eaten fresh, or are used to make fruit juice and wine. They can also be made into jellies and jams.

Raisins, sultanas, and currants, which are used for baking, are all different kinds of dried grapes.

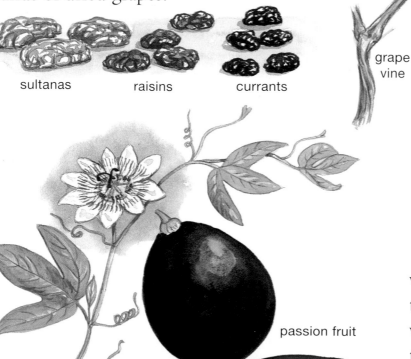

sultanas   raisins   currants

flowers

grape vine

grapes

passion fruit

Passion fruits grow on long vines. The egg-sized fruit has a tough skin that becomes wrinkled when it is ripe. Inside the fruit are the seeds. They are surrounded by a sweet, highly perfumed pulp. The flesh and the seeds are eaten together fresh, or are squeezed to make fruit juice.

The kiwi plant is covered with reddish hairs and has heart-shaped leaves. Male and female flowers grow on separate plants, so a pair must be planted to obtain fruit. The brownish furry fruit contains a sweet green pulp and black seeds.

Kiwi fruits that are going to be exported are picked while they are still hard. They keep well, and they ripen slowly, so they are ready to eat when they arrive in the shops.

kiwi fruit

Fruit facts

Grapes were grown by the Egyptians more than 6,000 years ago.

Passion fruits were first grown in Brazil.

Kiwi plants were first grown in China. They were once known as Chinese gooseberries. About 50 years ago, they were grown as a fruit crop in New Zealand. Since then they have been called kiwi fruit.

Fruit for breakfast

Raisins and sultanas taste good with nuts and cereals such as oats. They are often added to granola, but you can stir them into oatmeal as well.

1. Choose one of these fruits to make your own fruit yogurt.

2. *Ask an adult* to use a sharp knife to cut the fresh fruit for you.

3. Wash a few seedless grapes in cold running water and dry them. Then cut them in half.

Peel a kiwi fruit and then cut it into thin slices.

Cut a passion fruit in half. Scoop out the pulp, juice, and seeds and mix them into a bowl of plain yogurt.

4. Stir the rest of the fruit into the bowl of plain yogurt.

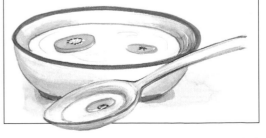

Mediterranean fruits

These fruits first came from the dry, sunny countries around the Mediterranean Sea. Now they are grown in warm areas all over the world.

Olive trees can grow on poor soil. They are often planted on hillsides in narrow strips of land called terraces. Olives are small, round, oily fruit with a hard pit in the middle. Green olives are picked half-ripe; black olives are the fully ripe fruit.

Olives can be eaten fresh or preserved in oil or salty water called brine. Some are used in cooked dishes such as pizza. Olives are also crushed to make olive oil, a healthy oil used for salad dressings and for cooking.

olives

fig

The flowers on a fig tree are unusual. They develop inside the fruit pulp. Ripe figs are purplish brown and soft. Inside there are many tiny seeds in a soft, sugary pulp. Figs are eaten fresh, or they are canned or dried to preserve them.

Date palms grow to 80ft (25m) tall and have separate male and female trees. Feathery flowers develop into huge bunches of dates. Soft dates are eaten fresh or are pressed into blocks used in baking. Hard, dry dates are ground into flour in Arab countries.

date palm

dates

pomegranate

The pomegranate is a small tree, 16ft (5m) high, with bright, orange flowers. The fruit has a tough outer skin filled with droplets of juicy pulp. Each droplet contains a hard seed. The fruit is eaten raw. The juice is used to make drinks.

Fruit facts

Olive trees can live for more than 1500 years.

Figs were one of the fruits most often eaten by the ancient Greeks and Romans.

Soft dates contain saccharine, which is sometimes used instead of sugar.

Granada means pomegranate. Granada in Spain was named after the tree.

Think green

Dates are often packed in long wooden or plastic boxes. You can reuse the boxes. Paint or cover the lids. Then use the boxes to store things such as pencils or jewelry.

Grow your own

Pomegranate

1. Collect some seeds from the fruit. Plant them in a pot of damp potting soil. Cover the pot with a plastic bag.

2. Leave the pot on a sunny window ledge. Remove the bag when the seedlings first appear.

3. Transplant the seedlings into a larger pot. Move the pot outside in the summer, but bring it inside during the winter.

Date palm

1. Remove some date pits (stones) from boxed dates. Soak the pits in warm water for two or three days.

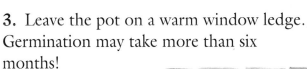

2. Plant the pits in a pot of damp potting soil. Cover the pot with a plastic bag.

3. Leave the pot on a warm window ledge. Germination may take more than six months!

Fig tree

Buy a plant or take fig cuttings. Some figs fruit very well in a greenhouse or a pot indoors. Other figs grow well outside if they are planted against a south-facing wall.

Fruits from many places

Ackee is an African tree that grows in the West Indies. The bright red fruits split open to show three black seeds, surrounded by white flesh. The white flesh can be eaten only when the fruit is ripe and open. Everything else is poisonous. Ackee fruits are eaten raw or cooked.

Guavas come from the Caribbean and South America. The green, yellow, or purplish pear-like fruits have pulpy flesh with many hard seeds. The flesh smells lovely, but sometimes it tastes bitter. Fresh or canned guavas are often cooked or made into jam.

ackee

litchi

Litchi, or lychee, come from southern China. The plants have long clusters of greenish flowers that produce bunches of warty brown fruit. Inside the hard rind there is soft white flesh and a shiny brown seed. Fresh or canned litchi can be eaten raw or cooked.

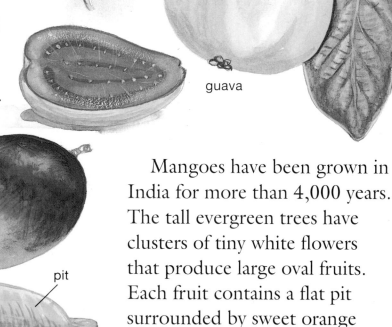

flower

guava

mango

pit

Mangoes have been grown in India for more than 4,000 years. The tall evergreen trees have clusters of tiny white flowers that produce large oval fruits. Each fruit contains a flat pit surrounded by sweet orange flesh. Mangoes are eaten fresh or canned. They are also used to make jams and chutneys.

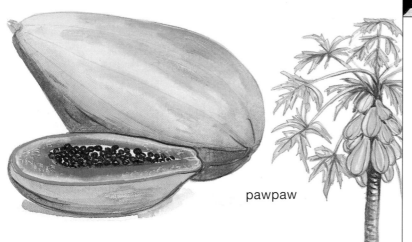
pawpaw

litchi

Grow your own

1. Take the seeds from fresh mangoes, pawpaws, or litchis and quickly plant them in a pot of potting soil.

2. Cover the pot with a plastic bag and leave it in a warm place.

3. Remove the plastic bag when the seedlings appear and put the pot in a warm, sunny place inside.

Pawpaws, or papayas, come from Central America and are grown in many tropical countries. The plant has a tall stem with leaves at the top. The melon-like fruits that grow from the stem have sweet orange flesh, with black seeds in the center. The seeds are peppery and cannot be eaten. Pawpaw plants grow very quickly from seed. They will start to fruit after only nine months.

persimmon

Persimmons, also called Sharon fruit, grow wild in North America. The fruits look like large orange tomatoes but grow on trees that are 60 ft (20m) tall. The fruits are bitter unless they are very ripe. They can be eaten raw, or cooked.

Rhubarb is not a true fruit at all. It is a leaf stalk, which is cooked and eaten like a fruit and is also used to make jam. It was first grown in Northern Europe as an herb for medicine.

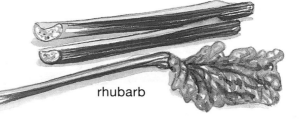
rhubarb

star fruit

Star fruits, also called carambolas, come from Indonesia. The long yellow fruits grow on small evergreen trees. The fruits are eaten raw in salads or cooked to make jams. When the fruits are cut across, they are star-shaped.

Glossary

acidic: sour or bitter, containing acid.

cane: the woody stalk of a fruiting plant, as the raspberry.

citrus: fruits such as lemons, limes, oranges, and grapefruit that contain citric acid.

compost: a mixture of decaying plant material, such as leaves, used to enrich soil.

cross: growing a plant or fruit from two different parent plants.

cultivate: to grow on a farm or in a garden.

cutting: a piece of plant stem that grows into a new plant.

distill: to heat and then cool a liquid until there is less of it, but its flavor is stronger.

drupelet: a small part or section of fruit flesh, containing seeds.

environment: everything around us, such as air, water, and land.

enzyme: chemicals in a living thing, which make other chemicals work.

export: to send goods for sale from one country to another.

ferment: when sugar in fruit changes into alcohol during wine making or when food rots.

germinate: when a seed starts to grow into a plant.

hemisphere: one half of the earth.

herb: a plant that does not have a woody stem and that dies down to the ground each year.

mold: to make something into a shape.

pollination: when the fertilizing powder called pollen is carried from one plant to another, so that the seeds can grow into fruit.

preserve: food that has been treated so that it does not go bad.

pulp: the juicy flesh of a fruit.

recycle: make something new from something that has already been used.

season:	the time during the year when a plant usually produces fruit.
segment:	a part or portion that is cut off or separated from the whole fruit.
starch:	a white food substance without taste or smell, which is in foods such as potatoes and bananas.
sucker:	a shoot that grows from the base of a plant stem or from a plant root.
tendril:	the long, stem-like part of a climbing plant that clings onto anything close to it, to help support the plant.
transplant:	to replant in another place.
tropical:	from the lands near the middle of the earth, where the heat from the sun is strongest. We draw lines on maps to show the position of the tropics. Tropical fruits grow best in hot, wet places.
variety:	a type of plant or fruit.
vitamins:	the small amounts of different substances in foods that people and animals need for good health. Most fruit contains vitamin C.
zest:	the thin layer of skin on the outside of an orange or lemon.

Further reading

Eat Well by Miriam Moss. Crestwood House, 1993. Young readers will learn how to plan a diet to help them stay healthy and will get practical advice that can help them improve their confidence and well-being.

Food and Feasts: With the Aztecs by Imogen Dawson. New Discovery Books, 1995. This introduction to the ancient Aztec civilization examines the food the people ate, their customs, feasts and festivals, and includes a variety of authentic, delicious recipes.

Harvest Festivals around the World by Judith Hoffman Corwin. Julian Messner, 1995. This book describes how the harvest was and is celebrated around the world, includes facts about customs and ceremonies, and presents instructions for harvest projects, such as preparing tasty dishes for the family to enjoy.

Index of fruits